# Rock Cycles

Rebecca Harman

H **www.heinemann.co.uk/library**
Visit our website to find out more information about Heinemann Library books.

To order:
☎ Phone 44 (0) 1865 888066
🖹 Send a fax to 44 (0) 1865 314091
💻 Visit the Heinemann Bookshop at www.heinemann.co.uk/library to browse our catalogue and order online.

First published in Great Britain by Heinemann Library, Halley Court, Jordan Hill, Oxford OX2 8EJ, part of Harcourt Education. Heinemann is a registered trademark of Harcourt Education Ltd.

Editorial: Melanie Copland
Design: Victoria Bevan and AMR Design
Illustration: David Woodroffe
Picture Research: Mica Brancic and Helen Reilly
Production: Duncan Gilbert

Originated by Chroma Graphics (Overseas) Pte. Ltd
Printed in China by WKT Company Limited

The paper used to print this book comes from sustainable resources.

ISBN 0 431 01299 7
09 08 07 06 05
10 9 8 7 6 5 4 3 2 1

**British Library Cataloguing in Publication Data**
Harman, Rebecca
Rock Cycles: formation, properties and erosion (Earth's Processes)
552

A full catalogue record for this book is available from the British Library.

**Acknowledgements**
The Publishers would like to thank the following for permission to reproduce photographs: buyimage.co.uk **p.27 (Top)**; Corbis **p.19**, GeoScience Features **p.5 (left)**; GeoScience Features **p.5 (right)**; GeoScience Features **p.7**; GeoScience Features **p. 9 (top)**; GeoScience Features **p.13**, GeoScience Features **p.17 (left)**, GeoScience Features **p.17 (right)**; GeoScience Features **p.27 (bottom)**; Getty Images/PhotoDisc **p.28**; Science Photo Library/Simon Fraser **pp.18, 24**; Science Photo Library/Jim Reed **p.20**; Science Photo Library/Bernhard Edmaier **p.21**; Science Photo Library/2001 Orbital Imaging Corporation **p.22**; Science Photo Library/NASA **p.26**; Still Pictures/S.J. Krasemann **p.9 (bottom)**; Still Pictures/Gallen Rowell **p.11**; Howard Oakley **p.12**; Still Pictures/Raimund Frankin **p.14**; Still Pictures **p.15**; Still Pictures **p.23**; Still pictures **p.25**.

Cover photograph of Goosenecks, incised meanders of the San Juan river, Utah, USA reproduced with permission of Robert Harding.

The Publishers would like to thank Nick Lapthorn for his assistance in the preparation of this book.

# Contents

Words appearing in the text in bold, like this,
are explained in the Glossary.

# What are rocks?

Rocks are found all over the surface of the Earth. Uluru, the Grand Canyon, and Stonehenge are all examples of rocks. They are all made of different types of natural substances called **minerals**. There are three different types of rocks: **igneous rocks**, **sedimentary rocks**, and **metamorphic rocks**.

## What are igneous rocks?

Igneous rocks are formed from a hot material called **magma** that comes from below the Earth's surface. Over millions of years, the magma rises, cools, and hardens to form igneous rocks. This can happen either underground or at the Earth's surface, both on land and underwater.

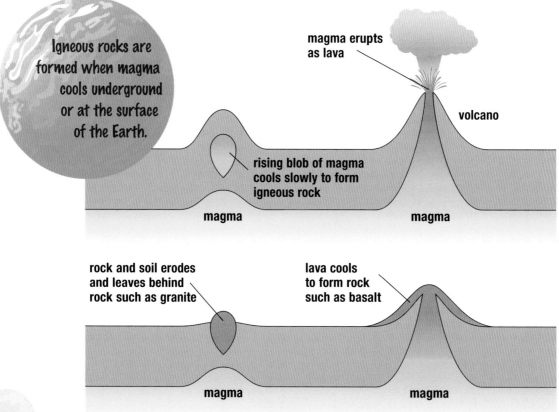

Igneous rocks are formed when magma cools underground or at the surface of the Earth.

magma erupts as lava

volcano

rising blob of magma cools slowly to form igneous rock

magma

magma

rock and soil erodes and leaves behind rock such as granite

lava cools to form rock such as basalt

magma

magma

If magma cools slowly underground, big mineral grains are formed and so the rock is **coarse grained**. Granite is an example of a coarse grained igneous rock. Granite appears at the surface of the Earth in some places, such as in Yosemite Valley, California, and Dartmoor, south-west England. This is because the soil and rocks above the granite have been **eroded**.

If magma rises all the way to the Earth's surface before it cools it is called **lava**. Sometimes this lava bursts through the surface in **volcanoes**. At the surface the lava cools quickly and **fine grained** rock, such as basalt, is formed. A large area of basalt, called the Columbia Plateau, covers most of the states of Washington and Oregon in the United States.

## Did you know?

**Most of the ocean floor is made of basalt, which comes from the eruption of underwater volcanoes.**

Both of these rocks are igneous. The granite (left) is coarse grained, while the basalt (right) is fine grained.

# What are sedimentary rocks?

Sedimentary rocks are formed from broken bits of other rocks.

When igneous rocks are attacked by wind and rain at the Earth's surface, tiny **particles** are broken off and carried by the wind or in rivers to other places. When the particles come to rest and pile up they are called **sediment**. Sediments are laid down in layers called beds. Over millions of years these beds are squashed as new sediment piles on top. This pushes the particles closer together. Some mineral grains act like cement, and stick the sediment together. This means that eventually new sedimentary rock is formed.

## Did you know?

- In areas where bits of mud and clay collect, they form a sedimentary rock called shale.

- In areas where sand collects, a sedimentary rock called sandstone is formed.

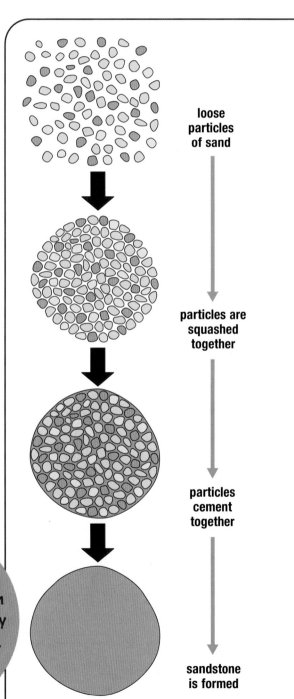

loose particles of sand

particles are squashed together

particles cement together

sandstone is formed

Over millions of years, loose sand can turn into a sedimentary rock called sandstone.

Some sedimentary rocks also contain parts of dead animals and plants, called **fossils**. Dinosaur fossils have been found in some rocks, and this is how we know they used to live on Earth. When tiny animals in the sea die, their bodies sink to the bottom and pile up into sediments. Over millions of years these are squashed to form sedimentary rock such as limestone.

As the beds in sedimentary rocks are laid down on top of each other, they record the passing of time. We can use the layers to estimate the age of the rocks. If they contain fossils, we can see how the plants or animals changed over time.

You can clearly see the dinosaur fossils in this sedimentary rock at Dinosaur National Monument in the United States.

# What are metamorphic rocks?

Metamorphic means changed. Metamorphic rocks are formed when heat or high **pressure** changes igneous or sedimentary rocks. This can happen in different ways.

When sedimentary rocks are buried deep under large layers of sediment (small pieces of rock and mud), they will experience an increase in pressure and will change into metamorphic rocks.

When hot magma rises below the Earth's surface it heats up the surrounding igneous rocks, just like baking them in the oven. These rocks will change into metamorphic rocks because of the increased heat.

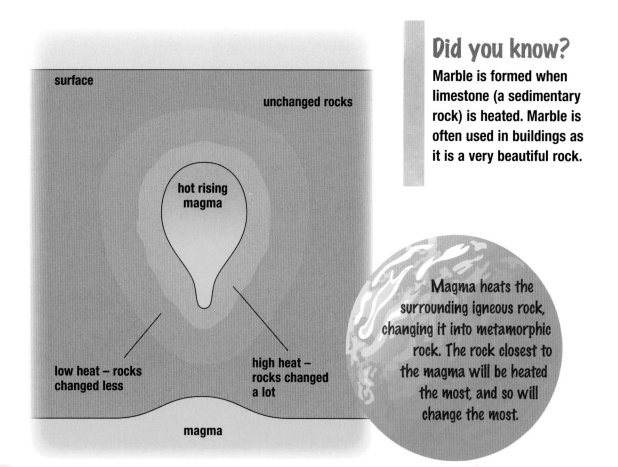

surface

unchanged rocks

hot rising
magma

low heat – rocks
changed less

high heat –
rocks changed
a lot

magma

## Did you know?

Marble is formed when limestone (a sedimentary rock) is heated. Marble is often used in buildings as it is a very beautiful rock.

Magma heats the surrounding igneous rock, changing it into metamorphic rock. The rock closest to the magma will be heated the most, and so will change the most.

When mountains are formed on Earth, the rocks are pushed upwards or buried under the growing mountains. This means they will experience high pressure and may be heated as well, so will change into metamorphic rocks. The Himalaya Mountains are made of metamorphic rocks.

Slate is formed when shale (a sedimentary rock) experiences high pressure under a mountain range. Slate is often used for roof tiles, as it can easily be split into thin layers.

Marble (top) and slate (bottom) are both metamorphic rocks.

# What is the rock cycle?

The surface of the Earth may seem as "solid as a rock" but, over many years, even the hardest rocks are worn away. There is a never-ending cycle of rock formation, break down (**weathering**), transportation (**erosion**), and settlement in a new place (**deposition**). All these processes make up what is called the **rock cycle**.

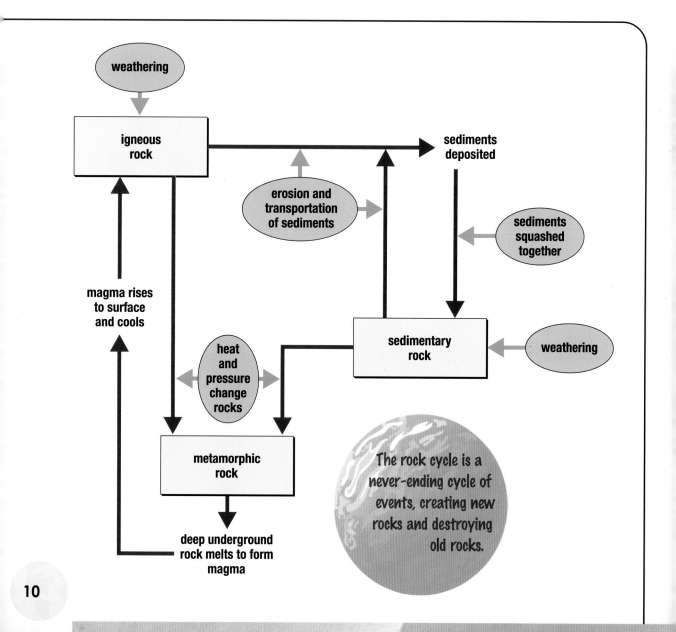

weathering

igneous rock

sediments deposited

erosion and transportation of sediments

sediments squashed together

magma rises to surface and cools

sedimentary rock

weathering

heat and pressure change rocks

metamorphic rock

The rock cycle is a never-ending cycle of events, creating new rocks and destroying old rocks.

deep underground rock melts to form magma

As soon as igneous, sedimentary, and metamorphic rocks are formed at the Earth's surface, they are attacked by the wind and rain. Over millions of years, bits of rock are chipped away in a process called weathering. These bits of rock are then transported away. They are taken to different places by the wind, rivers, or ice. This is called erosion. When the bits of rock can be transported no further, they are dumped in a new place. This is called deposition. Here the bits of broken rock settle to form sediments. As we have seen, over millions of years these sediments change into new rock, and the cycle can begin all over again.

The Grand Canyon in Arizona, USA was formed as rocks were worn away by the great power of the Colorado River, which flows through it.

# How are rocks broken down?

As soon as rocks are formed, the process of weathering starts to weaken the rock and break it down into smaller bits. Weathering is like using sandpaper to make a piece of wood smooth. The sandpaper grinds the surface down until it is flat, and tiny particles are produced.

On the Earth's surface, wind, water, ice, and chemicals (like acid in rainwater), split and **dissolve** the rock until it crumbles. Weathering affects statues, buildings, and anything else made of stone, as well as rocks. Where igneous rocks are formed underground they are protected from weathering. But once they reach the Earth's surface, as the rocks and soil above are eroded, the attack can begin.

This amazing rock in Australia, called Wave Rock, has been affected by physical weathering.

Weathering is a gradual process, and it takes place slowly over thousands of years. The speed of weathering depends on the type of rock. Most igneous and metamorphic rocks are more **resistant** to weathering than sedimentary rocks. This is because they are harder, and have fewer spaces between the mineral grains. Sedimentary rocks like limestone are less resistant so are more easily weathered.

There are two main ways in which rocks are broken down – **physical weathering** and **chemical weathering**. In physical weathering the rock is broken down without being changed. In chemical weathering, chemical reactions occur and these may change some of the mineral grains in the rock. Both types of weathering usually attack rocks at the same time.

The weathered rock on this mountain in Switzerland is called scree. It is formed by physical weathering.

# Physical weathering

There are many different types of physical weathering. These processes mainly take place in cold or dry places.

If rainwater gets into cracks in rocks and then freezes, it forces the rock apart because the water gets bigger as it freezes. This is called **frost shattering**. It happens in places where the ice melts in the day, and freezes again at night, such as in cold mountain regions. The cycle of freezing and thawing means that lots of rock is broken down in this way. The weathered rock that forms is called **scree**.

In dry places, such as deserts, salt crystals grow in the cracks in rocks. Just like ice, the salt forces the rock apart, and layers of rock peel off like an onion. This is called onion skin weathering.

When plant roots grow into cracks in rocks, they can cause the rock to break up. This happens a lot on pavements, where tree roots have lifted and cracked the paving stones.

These huge granite boulders in Australia are called "the Devil's Marbles". They are formed by onion skin weathering.

# Chemical weathering

Rocks can also be affected by chemical weathering. This form of weathering mainly takes place in hot and wet places. This is because water is needed for the chemical reactions, and the chemical reactions speed up when it gets hotter.

When rain falls on rocks, mineral grains in the rock may be dissolved by the water, like sugar in a glass of water. If the water is warm, the sugar will dissolve more quickly. In the same way, rock dissolves more quickly in hotter places, so this type of weathering is very effective in hot places where it rains a lot. When rainwater contains acid it can dissolve rock very quickly, especially limestone.

## Did you know?

**Rocks that contain iron may rust, just as something like a ladder, made from iron, rusts. Rusting is a chemical reaction that happens when iron reacts with air. It produces a red or brown stain on the rocks.**

This dramatic scenery is in China. It is formed by the chemical weathering of limestone.

# How does soil form from rocks?

**Soil** forms as weathering breaks rock down into smaller pieces. Air, water, and the rotting remains of dead plants and animals, called organic matter, fill the gaps between the bits of weathered rock. Once soil starts to form, the rock continues to be weathered. This is because the build-up of soil creates the perfect conditions for more weathering to take place. The water in soil can be very acidic, so the rate of chemical weathering will increase, and more soil will be produced.

## Did you know?

It takes from 100 to 1,000 years for 1 centimetre (0.4 inches) of soil to form. It will form much faster in hot, wet areas than in cold, dry areas. This is because chemical reactions are faster when it is hotter and there is plenty of water around.

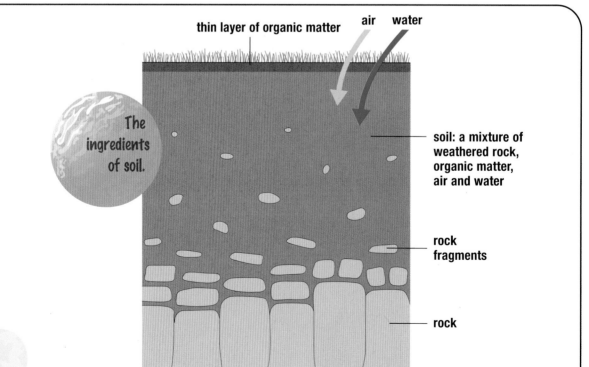

thin layer of organic matter    air    water

The ingredients of soil.

soil: a mixture of weathered rock, organic matter, air and water

rock fragments

rock

The type of soil that is formed depends mainly on the **climate**. The climate of an area is the type of weather it usually experiences. So if an area usually has a lot of rain, we say it has a wet climate.

In areas with hot, wet climates, such as the Amazon rainforest in Brazil, soils can form up to 30 metres (98 feet) deep. These are called ferralsols and they develop because of chemical weathering. In areas with dry climates, such as central Australia, only very thin soils less than 1 metre (3 feet) deep are found. This is because the rate of weathering is much slower. In areas with very cold climates, such as northern Canada, the soil may be frozen for much of the year. This type of soil is called tundra soil. Much of North America and Europe have dry summers and wet winters. The soils there are called chernozems and brown forest soils, and are usually about 2 metres (6.5 feet) deep.

Deep soils develop in the tropical rainforest (right), while very thin soils are found in deserts (left).

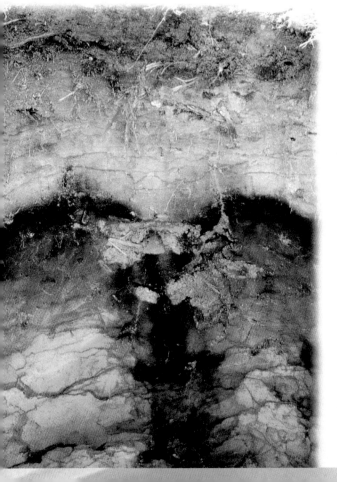

# How is weathered rock transported?

Weathering attacks rocks, and may completely destroy them. But in doing so it creates the materials to make more rocks. The removal of these broken bits of weathered rock by water, ice, and wind is called erosion. Weathering and erosion work together over millions of years to lower the surface of the land. They also make lots of material that will continue its journey through the rock cycle.

**Gravity** helps to speed up erosion on slopes. Loose, weathered rock will move downslope, just as a tennis ball will roll down a slope. This movement is often helped along by rainwater. Weathered rock moves downslope in different ways.

The slow movement of soil and weathered rock down slopes is called **soil creep**. The rate of movement is usually around 10 centimetres (4 inches) per year. This is too slow for us to see it happening. Sometimes the soil creeps a little faster. This will depend on the steepness of the slope, the type of weathered material, and the amount of rainwater on the slope.

Soil creep can speed up when the slope is very steep or if there has been a lot of rainfall.

If a lot of rain falls and soil and weathered rocks become full of water, they will be heavier, and will flow down the slope. This flow is rather like the flow of soggy porridge. It happens much faster than soil creep, at a rate of a few centimetres per day.

A sudden fast movement downslope, such as a **landslide** or a **rockfall**, may be caused by heavy rainfall or frost shattering. This movement can be over in a few seconds, but it can transport hundreds of tonnes of rock over hundreds of metres. Scree slopes form as the fallen material builds up.

This rockfall in Pakistan in 1990 has covered over the hiking path.

Weathered rock can also be transported by rivers, **glaciers**, or wind. These are the three main forces of erosion on the Earth's surface.

## Rivers

In a river, water runs within a channel and flows downslope towards the ocean. Erosion takes place in three main ways along a river.

1. **The force of the flowing water wears away loose, weathered rock from inside the river channel and carries it away. As the rocks are transported, they become smooth as they bash into and rub against each other.**

2. **Bits of rock carried by the river strike the sides and bottom of the channel and grind the rocks away. This is called abrasion.**

3. **The river water can also dissolve some of the rock in the river channel.**

All this means that the river carries lots of sediment – this is called its **load**. A fast-flowing river may be cloudy as it has a lot of energy and can carry a big load. A slow-moving river has less energy and cannot carry as much sediment.

This river has a lot of energy and is carrying a big load of sediment. It will cause a lot of erosion.

# Glaciers

Glaciers gradually move downslope, bulldozing everything in their path. They move at different speeds in different places. In the Alps, glaciers move about 40 metres (131 feet) per year. In Greenland, glaciers may move up to 1.5 kilometres (1 mile) per year.

As glaciers move, they pluck weathered bits of rock from the ground and carry them away. Glaciers are so powerful they can even carry rocks the size of houses. Frost-shattered rocks may fall on to glaciers from the mountainsides and become trapped in the ice. Glaciers and their rocky loads act like sandpaper, scratching and scraping the rock underneath as they move downslope.

## Did you know?

Glaciers are very slow-moving rivers of ice. They form when snow collects high in the mountains and hardens to form ice. Glaciers are found in cold countries such as Greenland and Iceland, and high in the mountains in places such as Alaska in the United States and the Alps in Europe.

This is the Turner Glacier in Alaska. You can see the rocks trapped in the ice.

# Wind

Wind is a weak force of erosion, when compared to rivers and glaciers. But it is important in deserts where there is very little water to hold the rock sediment together. Wind can only pick up and carry loose specks of rock that are about the same size as dust. But it can hurl them far across the landscape, sometimes for thousands of kilometres. The wind and its load of dust blasts against desert rocks and wears them down.

When larger grains of sand are blown by the wind, they skip across the land surface, but cannot be carried long distances. This is called saltation. Tiny pebbles will roll or slide, but are too heavy to be picked up, even by the strong winds of a dust storm.

This satellite image shows huge amounts of sand blowing from the Sahara Desert in Africa.

# What landforms are created by erosion?

Over much of the Earth, rivers, glaciers, and the wind are responsible for shaping the landscape. Many of the landforms we see around us are created by erosion.

## Rivers

Over thousands of years the steep, upper parts of rivers cut deep V-shaped valleys into the landscape. Further downstream they carve out much wider valleys as the river meanders (bends) from side to side across the valley floor. A waterfall may form when a river flows over hard rock onto softer rock. The river will erode the soft rock faster, forming a waterfall such as Niagara Falls in North America.

In their upper parts rivers carve V-shaped valleys into the landscape.

# Glaciers

High in the mountains, at the top of the glacier, the mountain peaks are sharpened into narrow ridges called **arêtes**, and pinnacles called **horns**, for example, the Matterhorn in Switzerland.

As a glacier flows downhill it widens, deepens, and straightens the valley it is travelling in. This creates a deep, U-shaped valley called a glacial trough. When the glacier scrapes over rocks, scratches called striations are formed. These can be seen in the rock once the ice melts. There are some striations in Central Park in New York, which formed 10,000 years ago underneath a glacier.

Hard, resistant rocks are not eroded but are **streamlined** by glaciers. This produces landforms called **roche moutonnées**. These range in size, and can be up to 100 metres (328 feet) long. They can be found in places such as Snowdonia in North Wales in the United Kingdom.

This valley in Greenland is an example of a wide U-shaped valley, about 1 kilometre (0.6 miles) deep. It was formed by the passage of a glacier.

# Wind

The wind blasts sand grains against desert rocks and makes them into unusual shapes. If harder rock lies on top of softer rock, this may result in mushroom-shaped rocks called pedestal rocks. Very smooth pebbles that have been abraded by the wind are called ventifacts. They are formed when the wind and dust attack the side of the pebble facing the wind.

This pedestal rock in Bolivia has been carved by the wind and dust into an unusual shape.

# How and where is weathered rock deposited?

After being worn away, transported by rivers, glaciers, or wind, bits of rock eventually settle down to rest. This is called deposition.

When rivers slow down, glaciers melt, or winds die down, the sediment they are carrying is dumped. Over millions of years, these sediments will change into new sedimentary rock, and the rock cycle will begin all over again.

Deposition in rivers mainly takes place in the lower parts of rivers. When a river bursts its banks and floods out over the valley floor it forms a wide, flat **floodplain**. Mounds of sediment dumped next to the river when it floods are called levees. When a river finally reaches the ocean or a lake, it will dump its load to form a delta. A delta is a muddy pile of sediment that looks like a giant fan from the air.

The rock material deposited by glaciers is called moraine. There are many different types of moraines, but they all form low hills or ridges. When moraine is deposited behind a lump of hard rock, it becomes streamlined to form a **crag-and-tail**. When huge boulders carried for kilometres by glaciers are dumped, they are called erratics.

A satellite image of the Lena River delta in Russia.

## Did you know?

Edinburgh Castle in Scotland is built on a crag-and-tail landform. The castle sits on the crag, and if you were to walk down the Royal Mile leading from the castle you would be walking along the tail.

Edinburgh Castle is built on a crag-and-tail landform.

In deserts sand is deposited in mounds called dunes. There are many different types of dunes. Sand may only remain on a dune for a short time before the wind picks it up and moves it again. In this way sand may be deposited in different places many times.

These huge sand dunes are in Algeria, northern Africa.

# Conclusion

The surface of the Earth is made up of three different types of rocks – igneous, sedimentary, and metamorphic. Over millions of years, these take part in a never-ending rock cycle where rocks are created, weathered, eroded, and deposited in a new place. Weathering and erosion work together to lower the surface of the land, and produce huge amounts of rock material to be recycled.

The three main forces of erosion on the Earth's surface are rivers, glaciers, and the wind. These help shape the landscape and produce landscape features. When rivers slow down, glaciers melt, or winds die down, the sediment they are carrying is deposited. Over millions of years, these sediments will change into new sedimentary rock, and the rock cycle can begin all over again.

A desert rock in Arches National Park in the USA.

# Fact file

These are some common minerals that make up rocks.

Biotite

Calcite

Diamond

Feldspar

Hornblende

Mica

Olivine

Pyroxene

Quartz

These are some common rock types.

| Basalt | A fine grained rock | Igneous |
|--------|--------------------|---------|
| Granite | A hard, coarse grained rock | Igneous |
| Obsidian | A black, smooth rock that looks like glass | Igneous |
| Pumice | A light rock with lots of holes in it like a sponge | Igneous |
| Limestone | A rock made from fossils on the ocean floor | Sedimentary |
| Sandstone | A rock made of sand | Sedimentary |
| Shale | A rock made from mud and clay that has layers in it | Sedimentary |
| Marble | A hard beautiful rock (limestone changed by heating) | Metamorphic |
| Slate | A hard, black layered rock (shale changed by pressure) | Metamorphic |

# Glossary

**abrasion**  bits of rock (in a river, glacier, or carried by the wind) striking other rocks and grinding them away

**acid water**  water with carbon dioxide dissolved in it; causes rapid chemical weathering of limestone

**arête**  narrow ridge formed by a glacier in mountainous regions

**chemical weathering**  breakdown of rock by chemical reactions

**climate**  type of weather an area usually experiences

**coarse grained rock**  rock containing big mineral grains

**crag-and-tail**  streamlined moraine (hill) behind a hard rock

**deposition**  laying down sediment in a new place

**dissolve**  when a substance mixes with water and becomes part of it

**erosion**  removal and transport of sediment

**fine grained rock**  rock containing small mineral grains

**floodplain**  wide, flat valley floor formed when a river floods

**fossil**  remains of a dead plant or animal

**frost shattering**  type of physical weathering where water freezes in cracks and breaks rock apart

**glacier**  slow-moving river of ice

**gravity**  force that makes things move downslope

**horn**  sharp peak formed by a glacier in mountainous regions

**igneous rock**  rock formed from magma either underground or at the Earth's surface

**landslide**  river of rocks flowing down a mountain very quickly

**lava**  name for magma when it reaches the surface of the Earth

**load**  sediment carried by a river, glacier, or the wind

**magma**  hot rock from below the Earth's surface

**metamorphic rock**  rock formed when igneous or sedimentary rocks are changed by heat or pressure

**mineral**  small, naturally occurring particle; rocks are made from lots of minerals

**particle**  tiny part of something

**physical weathering**  breakdown of rock without changing it

**pressure**  force acting on a rock, such as when sediments pile on top of it

**resistant**  more able to fight against something, for example, a rock being more resistant to weathering

**roche moutonnée**  rounded outcrop of rock formed by glacial weathering

**rock cycle**  unending cycle of rock formation, weathering, erosion and deposition

**rockfall**  rocks collapsing from a steep slope and moving downslope very quickly

**scree**  broken rocks formed by frost shattering on slopes

**sediment**  small pieces of rock and mud laid down

**sedimentary rock**  rock formed from the broken bits of other rocks

**soil**  mixture of weathered rock, air, water, and organic matter

**soil creep**  slow movement of soil and weathered rock downslope

**streamline**  in line with the direction of movement

**volcano**  mountain containing hot magma that erupts from time to time as lava

**weathering**  breaking down of rock

# Index

# More books to read

*Earth's Precious Resources: Rocks,* Ian Graham (Heinemann Library, 2004)
*I Was a Prehistoric Sponge,* Clay Cryute (Raintree, 2005)
*Rocks and Minerals series,* Melissa Stewart (Heinemann Library, 2002)
*Resources: Rocks, Minerals and the Environment,* Kathryn Whyman
(Stargazer, 2004)